CH

By the same author*

It Is Just You, Everything's Not Shit
21st Century Dodos
Harry Potter and the Order of the Phoenix
Ulysses
Roget's Thesaurus
The Highway Code
Gone Girl
Fifty Shades of Grey
Midnight's Children
The Gruffalo
The Pop-Up Kama Sutra

* OK, so I only wrote two of them, can you guess which two?

STEVE STACK

Christmas Dodos

Festive Things on the Verge of Extinction

The Friday Project
An imprint of HarperCollins*Publishers*
77–85 Fulham Palace Road
Hammersmith, London W6 8JB

(all cake to be sent to the above address)

www.harpercollins.co.uk

(not the best website, to be honest, you'd be better off visiting
www.facebook.com/hellofridayproject)

First edition published by The Friday Project in 2013

(unlikely to be a second edition unless you buy lots of copies)

Text copyright © Steve Stack 2013

(technically, yes, but if you want to nick anything to use on Facebook
or Twitter or to impress your friends I really don't have the legal clout
or motivation to do anything about it)

Steve Stack asserts the moral right to
be identified as the author of this work

ISBN: 978-0-00-752967-4

(no idea what this number means – try phoning it and see what happens)

Printed and bound in England by
Clays Ltd, St Ives plc

(I think someone in St Ives has been reading too much *50 Shades of Grey*)

MIX
Paper from
responsible sources
FSC C007454

FSC™ is a non-profit international organisation established to promote
the responsible management of the world's forests. Products carrying the
FSC label are independently certified to assure customers that they come
from forests that are managed to meet the social, economic and
ecological needs of present and future generations,
and other controlled sources.

Find out more about HarperCollins and the environment at
www.harpercollins.co.uk/green

For Mum and Dad

Contents

Foreword

What is a Christmas Dodo?

A Christmas Dodo is anything related to the festive season that is in danger of extinction. It might be a tradition that is going out of fashion or an item of food we associate with this time of year. It could be a classic toy or game that is becoming hard to find, or a once-shared experience unlikely to be shared again.

Wassailing, coffee creams, snowball fights in the school playground, paper chains and the *Blue Peter* advent crown – this book is full of such things. Many, sadly, are already effectively extinct, but there are some that are still around. For now.

I previously wrote a book called *21st Century Dodos*, which catalogued a veritable plethora of inanimate objects that could be classed as 'endangered', if anyone bothered to class such things. It sold some copies, and a number of readers suggested I pull together a festive version. Here it is.

If this book does nothing else, I hope it at least prompts you to pause and appreciate some of the items mentioned. Perhaps you will want to bid them a fond farewell, raise a glass of Harvey's Bristol Cream in their honour, or maybe, just maybe, make an effort to restore them to their former glory. Whatever your response, I hope you enjoy this nostalgic look at Christmas past.

STEVE STACK

21st Century Dodos

This book is essentially a festive extension of my last book, *21st Century Dodos*, in which I unearthed over 100 dodos from all walks of life – in the home, at school, at the cutting edge of technology, etc. *The Guardian* called it 'chummy 1970s and 80s nostalgia' which is probably about right. There is no need to have read that book before you read this one, but if you do buy both then I get more royalties and can afford a better class of biscuit to go with my many cups of tea.

Dodo Ratings

Every entry in this book is given a dodo rating of between one and five dodos. This indicates their rarity, ranging from one dodo (still quite common) to five dodos (completely extinct). If my last book is anything to go by then some readers will want to argue with me about the ratings I have allocated each item. Feel free, I love a good scrap. You can email me at 21stcenturydodos@gmail.com. I reply to every email I receive.

Contributors

Some of the entries in this book were suggested by other people via Facebook or Twitter. I have tried to keep dodo discussions going online and was delighted that so many people wanted to contribute ideas to a *Christmas Dodos* collection. Please feel free to join in the conversation; details of how to do so are at the end of the book. In the meantime, thanks to everyone who chucked ideas my way.

FOOD & DRINK

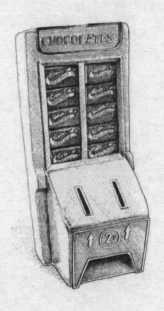

Coffee Creams

We all know that Coffee Creams (or Coffee Cremes, to use their official Cadbury's Roses title) were the worst chocolate in the tin [ducks as thousands of Coffee Cream fans hurl empty Caramel Barrel wrappers at him], so it was great news when they were discontinued [ducks again as a Caramel Velvet whizzes past his ear]. They join a long line of fillings and flavours that have been dumped, often after sitting happily in our Christmas tin of chocolates for many years.

Here are just a few examples:

Cadbury's Roses. Praline Moment, Lime Barrel, Montelimar, Coffee Creme, Almond Charm, Chocolate Bite, Chunky Truffle, Bournville, Orange Crisp, Noisette Whirl.

Quality Street. Apricot Delight, Chocolate Toffee Cup, Gooseberry Cream, Montelimar Nougat, Purple One (with brazil nut), Toffee Square, Peanut Cracknell, Milk Chocolate Round, Chocolate Strawberry Cream, Chocolate Truffle, Chocolate Nut Toffee Cream, Hazelnut Cracknell, Coffee Cream, Malt Toffee, Hazelnut Eclair and they even used to have mini-boxes of Smarties at one point.

Milk Tray. Apricot, Marzipan, Violet, Rosewater.

And then there are the selection boxes that are no longer with us either. Do you remember Week-End (chocolates and candies), Dairy Box, Terry's Moonlight, Black Magic and All Gold?

Suggested by Caroline Smailes

Dodo Rating: 🐦🐦🐦🐦🐦

Thruppenny Bits in the Pudding

Ah, that fine festive tradition of chipping your tooth on a thruppenny bit when tucking in to your Christmas pudding. This is now sadly on the wane, not least because there is no such thing as a thruppenny bit* any more.

It is seen as good luck to find the coin, although quite how it can be considered lucky to chomp down on a thick piece of metal, let alone at the risk of swallowing it, I have never understood.

The denomination of the coin has changed as the decades have rolled by, as well as being dependent on the affluence of the pudding maker, but it was usually of a relatively low value. Many families still follow the tradition – I suspect a pound coin is the new choking hazard of choice – but it is nowhere near as common as it once was, with the humble Christmas pud being under threat from Viennettas, Gu Chocolate Soufflés and puddings into which Heston Blumenthal has stuffed a whole orange and some Space Dust, or something like that.

Suggested by Vanessa Gebbie

Dodo Rating: 🐥🐥🐥

---

* *For those of a younger persuasion who have lived their entire lives in the decimal age, a thruppenny bit was the more common name for a 3p piece. Yes, we had a coin worth three pence in the olden days, just as we had coins worth six pence, half a pence and even a quarter of a penny. I talk about these, and other lost coinage, in* 21st Century Dodos.

Board Games on the Back of Selection Boxes

No Christmas is complete without a chocolate selection box: a variety of popular bars and other confections packaged in a cardboard box with a festive illustration on the front, which costs more than buying the contents individually. A simple con trick, which we happily fall for every year, because they make an easy present for nieces, nephews, godchildren, etc.

But why don't they have games on the back any more?

You could just about justify paying over the odds when you also got the pleasure of playing a board game using Chocolate Buttons or Jelly Beans or Tooty Frooties as counters. It might have been Snakes and Ladders or Ludo, or, better still, some contrived game involving characters featured on the sweet wrappers, perhaps a Freddo Frog lilypad race. Sadly, I haven't seen one of these for many a year.

I think they should bring them back.

And then someone should give me one for Christmas.

Suggested by Jacqueline Christodoulou

Dodo Rating: 🐦🐦🐦🐦

Dairy Milk Dispensers

There are but a select few presents that everyone, simply everyone, will have received at some point in their lives. The gift may differ depending on which decade you grew up in, but they all form a common link across each generation.

The legendary Dairy Milk Dispenser was one such item of my youth. This was a red plastic cabinet, which you filled with miniature Dairy Milk bars. These bars could then be removed by depositing a 2p piece in a slot, like a tiny vending machine. It was terribly exciting stuff – so exciting that none of us seemed to realise that we could have eaten all the chocolates without bothering with the dispenser. We were children deliberately making it more difficult for ourselves to get to sweets – unheard of at any other time of year.

Genius.

I was surprised to learn that these still exist today, but they are clearly not as popular as they once were, and they certainly don't take 2p pieces any more. It would appear to be 10p pieces these days, which is surely way above the rate of inflation?

Dodo Rating: 🐦🐦🐦

The Chocolate Junior
Smoker's Kit

In *21st Century Dodos* I wrote about a number of sweets and confections that had been hugely popular in days of old but are now frowned upon, or even banned, due to their connection with smoking. Even though there is not one shred of evidence that candy cigarettes, liquorice pipes or sweet tobacco encouraged anyone to start smoking the hard stuff when they were older they are now as hard to buy in your local newsagent as Spangles, Pacers or copies of *The Dandy*.

I was unaware, until it was mentioned to me by author Jonathan Pinnock, that there was a remarkable Christmas variety pack of such delights known as the Chocolate Junior Smoker's Kit. It came in selection-box style packaging and consisted of five cigarettes, two cigars, a pipe, a box of matches and an ashtray, all of which were made of chocolate! Its existence has almost been completely forgotten. Try googling it and you'll see how few entries come up, and most of these are just passing references. There is, however, one rather grainy photograph of an original box with its contents intact, which may well prompt a sudden wave of nostalgia from fake smokers in their 40s and 50s. It appears to be the only image of the kit anywhere on the Internet.

Suggested by Jonathan Pinnock

Dodo Rating: 🐤🐤🐤🐤🐤

A Nice Bottle of Blue Nun

Blue Nun was the first table wine actively and aggressively aimed at the mass market. In 1984, 1.25 million cases were sold in the USA alone, with hundreds of thousands of bottles bought in the UK. Although now seen as a bit of a joke, a 70s throwback and not something a serious wine connoisseur would even sniff at, it did a perfectly decent job and was extremely popular from the 50s right up to the early 90s.

The secrets to its popularity were a) it was cheap, and b) it was quite versatile and could be drunk with any sort of food. As a result, millions of families cracked open a bottle on Christmas Day.

Other festive tipples that have fallen foul of modern fashion include Harvey's Bristol Cream, Pomagne (a light, fizzy cider marketed as an alternative to champagne) and Black Tower wine, all of which are still available if you want to re-enact the Christmases of your youth, this time taking the role of your parents.

Suggested by Trevor Johnson

Dodo Rating: 🐦🐦

Cheese Footballs

They had never been anywhere near actual cheese and didn't really look anything like a football but they were nevertheless called cheese footballs, and even though that isn't a particularly festive concept, they were often thrown in the Christmas shopping trolley by eager kids shouting 'Please mum, please, it's Christmas!' to be eaten by the handful during the holidays.

Still around but perhaps not quite the staple they were some years ago.

Suggested by Steve

Dodo Rating: 🦤🦤

Satsumas and Nuts
in Your Stocking

Most of us seem to keep up the tradition of a Christmas stocking. For those parents that leave the bulging hosiery at the end of their children's beds, a stocking can buy an extra few minutes sleep whilst the kids excitedly rip open their first presents of the day at 5am in the morning. Other children find their stocking waiting on the fireplace to be opened before breakfast. Many families *only* open the stocking presents on Christmas morning, saving those under the tree until after lunch or dinner.

Whenever and however you do it, or did it, the chances are that you remember getting a satsuma or a bag of nuts in your stocking, or some other simple food.

No one knows quite how this tradition began. Some historians suggest that when we first started filling our stockings at Christmas, the contents were predominantly foodstuffs – the aforementioned fruit and nuts along with small confections, pies and biscuits – so any edible items in our stocking today hark back to those times.

Of course, we are now more likely to have a Terry's Chocolate Orange in our stocking than a satsuma, or a bag full of chocolate coins rather than one of nuts, but it is pleasing to discover that some people still pop in something simple and inexpensive for old time's sake.

Long may it continue.

Dodo Rating: 🐦🐦

Newberry Fruits

There are many foodstuffs associated with the festive season. Some of these are obvious and the same for everyone: Christmas pudding (the clue is in the name), mince pies, brandy butter, and so on. Some are fairly common all year round, but increase in popularity as Christmas nears; how many of us have a bowl of nuts in the living room in any month other than December?

But others are particular brands or products that will mean nothing to many, but cause an overwhelming sense of nostalgia for certain people.

Sugared almonds do it for me. I only ever saw them at Christmas and even then only if we visited my grandparents' house. My grandparents kept sugared almonds in a little ceramic dish in their 'best room' and we would be allowed to take one if we'd been particularly well behaved.

Newberry Fruit Jellies, it seems, do it for many others, at least if the *21st Century Dodos* Facebook page is anything to go by. When compiling entries for this book I received many suggestions from readers, but this one got the most people salivating at the memory.

Newberry Fruits were sugar-coated luxury jelly sweets, that came in different fruit flavours – raspberry, lemon, orange, blackcurrant, lime and strawberry – all presented in a tray not unlike a box of chocolates. The sugar coating would form a hard crust and the jellies would unleash a liquid centre when bitten into, much to the delight of the eater.

Manufactured by Meltis in humble Bedford for decades, production moved to Germany in the 90s after which Newberry Fruits vanished from the UK market completely. They have staged a mini-comeback in the past decade but, according to many reports in online forums, they are not quite the same as they used to be.

But then again, what is?

Suggested by Paul Burden

Dodo Rating: 🐤🐤🐤

TRADITIONS

Yule Log

The chances are that when you think of a Yule log the picture in your head will be of a chocolate cake fashioned to look like a tree trunk. However, these are actually a recent invention, first made to replicate the real wooden logs to which most Western cultures attached great significance at Christmas time.

Although the specifics of the Yule Log tradition differs from country to country, the basic principles are the same: someone brings a massive log, or even a whole tree, into the house and it is burned to bring good luck to the family for the coming year.

Here are some of the variations:

UK. An entire tree is brought in and stuck into the fire, trunk first. The name differs from region to region. *Yule Clog*, *Yule Block*, *Y Bloccyn Gwylian* in Wales meaning the Festive Block, and, my favourite, *Yeel Carline* in Scotland, which means 'the Christmas Old Wife'.

Serbia. A young oak tree is felled on Christmas Eve and a log taken from it. This log, called a *badnjak*, is burned all through Christmas Day. The first visitor to the house on that day has to hit it with a poker and wish the family good luck.

Germany. The Christmas log is added to the fireplace on December 24th.

France. A similar tradition was followed in France as in Germany, but from the 1940s onwards it was replaced with the *Bûche de Noël*, the cake we all know as a Yule Log today.

Bulgaria. Here hosts one of the most convoluted Yule Log rituals. A young man dresses in his best clothes and goes out on Christmas Eve to chop down a pear, elm or oak tree, this is known as the *Budnik*. He must then carry the tree home without it touching the ground. Once he reaches the door of his house, he engages in a call-and-response with the family inside: 'Do you glorify the young god?' he asks three times, and on each occasion the family responds with 'We glorify him, welcome'. A hole is then drilled into the log and filled with a blend of incense, before being burned in the fireplace. In the morning, the fire is extinguished with wine and the ash and charred wood are used to bless the harvest for the coming year.

Catalonia. In my favourite of all the traditions, a log is wrapped in a blanket and fed grass for several days. On Christmas Eve it is spanked over and over again in order to make it poo presents.

It's not hard to work out why these traditions are dying off: we don't have fireplaces any more, at least very few of us do (as Santa himself can testify) and, to be honest, the chocolate versions are a lot less hassle and much, much tastier.

Still, I love the idea of hitting a log till it defecates a gift.

Suggested by Chris Nicholl

Dodo Rating: 🐥🐥🐥🐥

Watching the Queen's Speech

Lots of people still watch the Queen's Christmas Message when it is broadcast across the major terrestrial channels at 3pm on Christmas Day. In 2012, it was seen by 8.3 million. However, that was a jubilee year. The general trend is actually one of decline.

It used to be that the nation stood still to watch the Queen – some quite literally, with entire families standing up throughout the ten-minute broadcast – but today the programme is suffering from the same issue as all television: too many channels, too little time.

That 2012 viewing figure was the largest for some years, only 5.6 million tuned in in 2009 and by 2010 the Queen's speech had dropped out of the top ten most viewed completely. Even the 2012 figures are a huge drop on the 28 million who watched in 1987, the 12.8 million in 1997 and the 9.3 million at the turn of our new century.

Clearly, it will be around for years yet and is destined to become the King's Speech at some point in the future (no rush, Your Majesty!), but I doubt the overall downward trend will be arrested for some time.

So, not extinct, and perhaps not strictly endangered, but definitely becoming less important.

Dodo Rating: 🐦

Christmas *Radio Times*

When I suggested on Twitter that I might include this entry in the book, I was berated by friends who refused to accept that the Christmas edition of the *Radio Times* could possibly be considered endangered, let alone a dodo. After all, everyone buys a copy, don't they?

I accept that it remains very popular, with plenty of homes sporting a copy on the arm of the sofa as December draws on, but – and this is a big but – although lots of people buy it, I don't think many of them read it, let alone *use* it.

I had a copy last Christmas. I didn't even open it.

And why would I? I have a Sky+ box which has an electronic programme guide. I can scan every channel for a full week ahead, and decide what I want to watch and what I want to record. And if I do manage to miss anything, I can always watch it later on iPlayer or one of the other online catch-up channels.

As much as it pains me to say it, I just don't need the Christmas *Radio Times*.

Perhaps I should stay loyal to Auntie Beeb, that august and reliable broadcasting institution, but the thing is, the *Radio Times* is no longer owned by the BBC anyway, it was sold off in 2011. Moreover, it isn't even the most popular TV listings mag any more – with both *TV Choice* and *What's on TV* (a magazine I have never even heard of) selling more copies in an average week.

Though I would love it to continue printing forever, I fear that its future is in jeopardy as more and more people realise that, like me, they can live without it.

Dodo Rating:

Christmas Boxes

There are a number of theories as to where the name 'Boxing Day' comes from. One suggestion is that it refers to the small earthenware boxes that in medieval times the poor would use to store their savings, before smashing them open at Christmas in order to spend the money inside. Another is that traditionally the day after Christmas was when the lord of the manor or master of the house would hand out small cash gifts to his staff and servants, and that this is also the source of the 'Christmas box', a tip given to a range of service-people around the festive season. Even in regular households, the postman or postwoman, the kid who delivers the papers, the milkman, the butcher's boy, the pools collector (I am going back a bit here), and various other people who would regularly deliver or collect from your door would be given a small token of appreciation – a few quid, a bottle of wine, some homemade jam, or something like that. It was a simple 'thank you' for braving wind, rain, snow and sleet all year round and was, I think, a genuinely nice gesture.

Over the course of the day, a milkman, or whoever, could pocket a tidy sum, and a range of home-made goods, by the time he or she got to the end of their round on Christmas Eve. Bankers get their bonuses no matter what they do, it seems fair that those a bit further down the salary chain should do likewise.

But, as I discussed in *21st Century Dodos*, this tradition is rapidly dying out. One obvious reason is that very few of us have deliveries from the butcher or baker any more, pools collectors are no longer, and even milkmen are on the decline. The only regular door-to-door caller most of us receive is a postman, and nowadays they rarely call in the morning when everyone is in and routes can often be serviced by a variety of different staff. If I handed over a fiver to the postman who called on Christmas Eve it might be someone I have never met or spoken to before.

I suspect that once our current elderly generation dies off (no rush folks, happy for you to stick around for a while longer), this tradition will die off with them.

Suggested by Jo

Dodo Rating: 🦤🦤🦤🦤

Blue Peter Advent Crown

There goes John Noakes, wrapping wire coat hangers in tinsel, attaching some yoghurt pots and plonking four candles in them: creating the traditional advent crown, which would be copied by tens of thousands of children up and down the land, and scare the bejesus out of their parents when the kids actually insisted on lighting it.

This major fire hazard was a staple of BBC children's television for decades, and for many it marked the beginning of the festive period. The design changed slightly each year (and, yes, I know it never actually included yoghurt pots), but central to all were wire coat hangers and tinsel even after both items had fallen out of fashion. Remarkably there are no recorded deaths from fire caused by the advent crown.

In 2010, the traditional crown was replaced by an elaborate and ill-judged 'chain reaction machine' which, bizarrely, involved the burning of both a crown and the *Blue Peter* badge.* Obviously this had middle-England up in arms and Anthea Turner spoke for them all when she said 'The advent crown is part of the bricks and mortar of what makes *Blue Peter* so special. To burn it is sacrilege. It was a wonderful tradition and both children and adults loved making it. What are they trying to prove?'

Suggested by Tim Footman

Dodo Rating: 🐦🐦🐦🐦

---

* *Well, according to the* Daily Mail *it did.*

Fairy Lights on the Blink

Now, before you shout at me because your fairy lights didn't work yet again this Christmas, I'm not lying when I say this classic festive gripe could soon be a thing of the past – and, indeed, already would be if you bothered to ditch your ancient set and shell out for a brand new one.

It is a timeless scene: mum or dad spending hours unravelling the tangle of lights from last year, winding them around the tree, knocking it off its axis while doing so, only to switch them on to discover they aren't working, and giving a cry of 'Buggeration!' or some such acceptable swear word.

The reason for this problem was the fact that fairy lights used to be filament bulbs on a series circuit. Filament bulbs had a tendency to blow with some regularity, especially if manhandled on and off the tree every year, and a series circuit meant that if one bulb blew then the whole set of fairy lights stayed obstinately unlit.

But that wasn't all! There was no way of working out which bulb had gone without checking every single one, and even if you could find it, it was rare to have a replacement with which to fix it. Many of you will have witnessed a parent close to tears as they dismantled all the tree decorations and drove down to Woolworths to buy a brand new set.

But this scene should be a thing of the past. Modern fairy lights use LED bulbs and work on a parallel circuit arrangement so they are far more reliable and much easier to fix if something goes wrong. All you need to do is chuck out those old ones and a stress-free Christmas is guaranteed.*

Dodo Rating: 🐤🐤🐤🐤

---

* *Not actually guaranteed.*

Having Time off Work

Christmas used to be the one holiday observed by the whole nation. With the exception of the emergency services and a small number of essential workers, pretty much everyone was off work for a couple of days.

But this has changed in recent years, especially when it comes to Boxing Day. It is hard to think of a shop, restaurant, etc. that isn't open on December 26th, and these places need staff.

Now, the people rushing to their local branch of Gap to pick up a cheap pair of pants are probably delighted to find the door open, guarded by one of those greeters ('Hello, how are you today?') and the shop full of staff constantly folding and refolding jumpers, but I for one think it further erodes the magic of Christmas.

The festive holiday is gradually being reduced to just one day. It wouldn't surprise me if the Next sale were to start at 3pm on Christmas Day in a few years' time.

Some call it progress. I call it one more day of shopping that none of us really need. Sit back, have another Bailey's, pop a mince pie in your mouth, watch a movie. Do anything, just don't go out.

Keep Christmas special.

Dodo Rating: 🐦🐦🐦🐦

Santa Bringing All the Gifts

I don't know about you, but when I was growing up Santa was responsible for all the presents we received at Christmas: the odds and sods in the stocking (including the satsuma, a fruit I understand to be bountiful at the North Pole), the gift-wrapped boxes under the tree, and the occasional unwrapped one that appeared towards the end of the day because 'Father Christmas must have dropped this on his way out'.

The only exceptions were the gifts from friends and relatives that were clearly labelled 'To Steven, with love from your Great Aunt Ivy xx' and so on, most of which were shaped like Parker pen boxes or Ladybird books. These were, allegedly, *delivered* by Santa but not actually *from* him.

This meant that there were no presents specifically from my parents and, as I recall, this arrangement was very common amongst families at the time, although with a number of slight variations. Some parents kept up the full Santa pretence including the ridiculous notion that everything under the tree was manufactured by elves even if they were clearly made by Mattel, Ideal or Waddingtons, others claimed that they chose all the presents and the jolly bearded chap just handled the delivery (and to be fair he was far more reliable than Yodel and DHL are today).

Of course, none of this mattered once the children realised that it was a whopping big lie, a realisation that could be prompted by many things: schoolmates proclaiming 'you don't still believe that, do you?'; a noisy parent tripping over a Tonka toy while depositing the stocking; the realisation that your house does not contain a fireplace; or, in the case of a family friend, the child saying in tears 'I got lots of lovely presents from Santa but nothing from you, mummy and daddy' only for mummy to exclaim in exasperation 'they are all from us, Santa doesn't exist!'. At which point Christmas loses some of its wonder, especially once you realise that the present Santa 'dropped on his way out' is actually something your parents forgot to wrap during a hectic Christmas Eve.

Nowadays it seems that most parents adopt a more pragmatic approach. I conducted an unscientific straw poll on Twitter and discovered that most now tell their kids that Santa brings the stocking presents (or pillow-case presents in particularly affluent houses), but the rest are all from mummy and daddy/mummy and mummy/daddy and daddy.*

This probably makes more sense, and saves a lot of uncomfortable questions, but is, if you ask me, a tad less magical.

Dodo Rating: 🐤🐤🐤

---

* *Delete as applicable.*

Everything Being Closed

If you are reading this on Christmas Day (and if you are, I must congratulate the person who gave you my book as a gift on having such fine taste), the chances are that if you run out of milk, have forgotten to stock up on gravy granules, or you're in need of a good stuffing then you could pop out to a shop nearby and pick up the item you require. Somewhere in the vicinity there will be a corner shop or a newsagents or even a small supermarket that will be open.

This was not always the case. Far from it. Until relatively recently everything, with the exception of hospitals, police stations, taxi companies, service stations, pubs and hotels (feel free to let me know if I have forgotten anything), was closed on Christmas Day. If you were out of an essential item, there was nothing you could do about it, unless a friendly neighbour was prepared to let you have some.

Things are very different now. Sure, your local high street (assuming you still have one) will be pretty much deserted, but most of us will be able to find somewhere selling what we need and when we get there we'll meet a small number of mildly embarrassed shoppers and share a knowing smile with them.

The major reason for this development is that lots of shopkeepers and, it should be noted, lots of customers don't celebrate Christmas at all, something we conveniently forget when caught up in the hype around the festive season and the frenzied shopping chaos leading up to the big event. Although the UK is notionally a Christian country it is full of people of other races, cultures and religions, and some of them are, thankfully, more than happy to sell us a packet of butter on Christmas Day.

Dodo Rating: 🐤🐤🐤🐤🐤

Wassailing

When was the last time you saw someone wassailing? Or went wassailing yourself? Do you even know what wassailing is? I didn't before I sat down to write this entry.

There are actually two distinct types of wassailing, both of which hark back to pre-Christian times, having their roots in pagan celebrations: the house-visiting wassail, a somewhat more rowdy forerunner to carol singing; and the orchard-visiting wassail, a traditional rite carried out around Christmas time in apple orchards.

House-visiting wassailing was most popular in medieval times, when feudal lords would give peasants some food and drink in exchange for a blessing. This developed a sinister edge over the years, ending up with gangs of drunken men bothering householders for free food, and if they didn't get any they would often break in and take it themselves. This adds a certain threatening tone to the request for figgy pudding in 'We Wish You a Merry Christmas': 'We won't go until we get some, so bring some out here.'

The orchard-visiting wassail was far more pleasant and involved a celebration of drink and song, designed to bless the trees and ensure a good apple harvest and lots of cider in the coming year. The gathered crowds would bang pots and pans and sing heartily to 'wake the trees':

Wassaile the trees, that they may beare
You many a Plum and many a Peare,
For more or lesse fruits they will bring,
As you do give them a Wassailing.

Thankfully, the house-visiting wassail has evolved into the (usually) more harmless carol singing, but deep in the West Country, the orchards still resound to the merry noises of wassailing to this day.

Dodo Rating: 🦤🦤🦤

Carol Singers

As a youth I distinctly remember that in the run up to Christmas there would be several knocks upon our door. Opening up we would be greeted by a variety of carol singers, from members of the church choir, all in good voice and collecting for the roof fund or the local poor, to a bunch of scruffy oiks trying to scrape together enough money for a packet of JPS or a bottle of shandy with a dodgy and unenthusiastic rendition of 'We Wish You A Merry Christmas'.

If we had actually had any figgy pudding I am sure we would have brought some out to them. Instead I think we handed over loose change and went back to watching *Ask The Family*.

Today you are more likely to stumble over a group of carol singers in the concourse of your train station or outside Marks & Spencer on a late shopping night in December than you are on your doorstep. I live on a residential street in the middle of a town and I have not had a single bunch of carol singers knock on my door in the past decade; speaking to others it does seem that the door-to-door carol delivery service is indeed a bit of a rarity these days.

I assume this is partly down to the reticence of parents when it comes to allowing their kids to go out knocking on strangers' doors during the hours of darkness. This I can understand, but it is a shame that a pretty harmless, if not always very tuneful, tradition is dying out because of our often-misplaced fears concerning the kindness of others.

Dodo Rating:

The Word 'Christmas'

The problem with the word 'Christmas' is that it contains the word 'Christ'. This is, it must be said, quite a big selling point for Christians, but has also caused issues for some local authorities worried about offending people of other faiths. These authorities have, instead, looked for a less troublesome word for the festive period such as, you've guessed it, Winterval.

The result was, of course, that they ended up offending lots of Christians, which is quite funny when you consider that most Jews, Muslims, Hindus, Scientologists and whoever else weren't remotely bothered about the word 'Christmas' in the first place.

In America they avoid the whole problem by wandering around wishing everyone 'Happy Holidays', thereby covering all bases since pretty much every religion has a festival around that time and atheists are just pleased to have a few days off. Everyone's happy.

Dodo Rating: 🐦🐦

No Contact

Christmas Day used to be the one day of the year when you could pretty much guarantee no one would bother you. Well, apart from the relatives you had to spend the day with, and perhaps the occasional phone call.

We don't even have to go back twenty years to find a time before emails, before texts, before instant messaging. It can be hard to recall what it was like back then, even if you are old enough to do so (and let's be honest, if you are reading this book you probably are). This was a time when, if you wanted to contact someone on Christmas Day, you picked up the phone and called them. That was it. No other options. You couldn't use Skype, you couldn't tweet them, you couldn't send them an Instagram photo of your roast dinner.

Today you can share your festive celebrations with the world, in real time, via Facebook and Twitter and a host of other services. There are many advantages to this, obviously, and to most it makes the whole thing a bit more special.

To antisocial blighters like me, it's just one more thing that makes it less so.

Dodo Rating: 🐤🐤🐤🐤🐤

Ashen Faggot

This was a tradition peculiar to the south west of England – similar to the Yule log, but with a bit of wassailing thrown in for good measure.

A bundle of ash twigs would be bound together with green ash withies and thrown on the fire. As the withies would burst and crack (green fresh wood tending to make rather a lot of noise as it burns) the party would toast each one with a drink. In some versions of the tradition, young ladies of the party would each select a withy and the first to crack would indicate marriage for that woman in the coming year.

Once the bundle had collapsed and the twigs had started to burn, some twigs would be removed in order to be used in the middle of next year's ashen faggot (also known as an ashton fagot).

I am delighted to report that this tradition is still upheld in at least one place. The landlords of the Harbour Inn in Axmouth, Devon make a giant ashen faggot every year and burn it in the pub fireplace.

Dodo Rating:

End of Term Parties

When I was at school, the last day of every term was a celebration; true for teachers as much as pupils, both delighted to be seeing the back of each other for a few weeks. Kids didn't have to wear their uniforms and were often allowed to bring a game in (I remember a particularly epic session of Test Match in 1978).

And, at Christmas there was often the added bonus of a class party: sausages on sticks, cheese and pineapple hedgehogs, sandwiches with the crusts cut off, fairy cakes with dribbles of icing, jam tarts and, if you were very lucky, oblong slabs of ice cream shoved into stale box-shaped wafers. All previous bullying, arguments, petty squabbles, cliques and hierarchies were forgotten for an hour or two while everyone, dressed in their civvies, tucked in to a festive feast.

These parties were special because of their rarity. Nowadays it seems that hardly a fortnight goes by without a Jeans for Genes day, or a mufti day for Comic Relief, or a cake sale, a pyjama day or some other reason for kids to dress down, stuff their faces or enjoy some sort of relaxation of the rules.

I prefer the old ways, antiquated though they may be.

Suggested by Jo

Dodo Rating: 🐤🐤🐤🐤

CHRISTMAS PRESENTS

Parker Pens

No Christmas in the '60s, '70s or '80s would have been complete without a Parker pen. At the time, most of us had never heard of Mont Blanc, Caran D'Ache or Sheaffer, and a Parker pen was the height of writing luxury.

The pen you unwrapped on Christmas morning, housed in its distinctive box – transparent lid, pen resting in a velvet-effect base – was almost certainly purchased by an elderly relative at the pen counter of their local WH Smith. Yes, so popular were Parker pens that they were displayed beneath a glass counter in a separate section of the shop, often alongside an array of scientific calculators and some posh compass and protractor sets.

I had always assumed that Parker pens were an ancient British institution, and it is true that they were produced in Newhaven in Sussex for many years, but the original Parker was actually an American. George Safford Parker founded the Parker Pen Company in 1888 in Janesville, Wisconsin. Parker had been working as a sales agent for another pen company before founding his own. He patented his first fountain pen in 1889 and went on to introduce a number of innovations to the industry, including a type of quick drying ink that removed the need for blotting paper. This is the product we now know as Quink. The Parker 51, introduced in 1941, became the best selling fountain pen in history. The Parker Pen Company itself was one of the top two in its field from the 1920s right up to the end of the '60s when the invention of the disposable ballpoint changed the face of writing instruments forever. Nonetheless, Parker pens remained extremely popular and were the gift of choice for grandmothers and great aunts doing their Christmas shopping every year.

Following a number of acquisitions of other companies, the Parker Pen Company was itself bought by Gillette in the '90s and then sold on to Newell Rubbermaid in 2000 where it now resides alongside fellow writing brands such as Sharpie, PaperMate and Waterman.

In 2009, Newell Rubbermaid announced the closure of operations in Janesville after more than 125 years. The Parker brand lives on, however, and if you are very lucky you might receive one of their pens in your stocking this Christmas.

Dodo Rating:

Ideal Toys

Most of us will have personal memories of the games and toys we once received and played with at Christmas time, and no list could possibly capture them all. I vividly remember a game that involved trying to fit different shaped plastic pieces into holes in a board before the whole thing popped up, flinging the pieces all over the place. It was, appropriately enough, called *Frustration*. Then there was *Mouse Trap*, a game that took so long to set up that by the time you had done so your mum would call you down for dinner so it never got played all the way through. You will have your own examples, I am sure.*

One company was responsible for many of the best-selling toys and games of the '60s, '70s and '80s: Ideal Toy Company. Ideal was founded in the early 20th century and are credited as the inventors of the teddy bear as well as a string of other dolls, including Evel Knievel and Shirley Temple figures. However, in the UK, it was their toys and games that they were famous for.

Here are just a few of their products:

Buck-a-roo! Load various Wild West paraphernalia onto a temperamental donkey until it gets so fed up it kicks its hind legs and throws everything skywards.

---

* *One place full of such examples is* TV Cream Toys *by Steve Berry, a book that features pretty much every toy and game of yesteryear you can imagine, including some that you will have completely forgotten.*

The Dukes of Hazzard Racing Set. Scalextric rip-off with cars from the popular redneck TV show.

Gaylord the Walking Basset Hound. Not sure he would get off the drawing board today, but Gaylord was a battery-powered plastic dog complete with magnetic bone and a box that doubled up as a kennel.

The Great Escape. Not a spin-off from the war movie but a 3D board game in which players had to escape from jail.

I Vant to Bite Your Finger. Make your way around this graveyard board game, but don't land on certain squares or you have to put your finger in Dracula's mouth – if it comes out with fang marks then you have to return to the beginning. *Twilight* fans should demand it make a comeback.

KerPlunk. Straws. Marbles. A transparent tower. Hilarity ensues.

Rebound. Ping little ball bearings encased in plastic up against a rubber band in the hopes of getting them into the scoring zone. A bit like miniature indoor curling.

Tin Can Alley. Shoot cans with a rifle that emits a harmless light beam.

A series of takeovers and mergers beginning in the early '80s led to the Ideal brand being subsumed into others. The UK arm of the company was taken over by Hasbro in 1997; some of their better-known products still sell under the MB Games brand.

Suggested by Trevor Johnson

Dodo Rating: 🐤🐤🐤🐤

Games
Compendiums

Or is it compendia?

Whatever the plural, we all remember these: dozens of popular board and card games condensed into one box. Endless hours of fun, surely?

Compendiums were often at the very budget end of budget games – made out of flimsy cardboard, they required multiple use of the same boards and counters. However, they did, just about, do what they said on the tin, as it were.

You'd have a chequered board, which served for both chess and draughts – the flat chess pieces sometimes needing to be pushed out of perforated cardboard. On the reverse might be a Snakes & Ladders board or Back-gammon or perhaps Ludo. There would also be smaller boards for Tic-tac-toe (using the black and white plastic draught pieces as counters) and other such games, and perhaps a pot for Tiddlywinks. A pack of cards could increase the number of possible combinations consider-ably, and there would often be rules for peculiar games that no one had ever heard of before. Or since.

It was a neat idea, but the reality was that it was only a temporary distraction. A few lost pieces or a spilled glass of weak lemon squash and the whole thing was ruined.

I've not seen one of these on sale anywhere for donkey's years. I suspect they still exist, but they are, I am sure, worthy of inclusion on our endangered list.

Suggested by Nasim Marie Jafry

Dodo Rating: 🐤🐤🐤

Ronco Records

Named after its founder, Ron Popeil, Ronco sold a range of products via TV ads in the '70s. Many of their lines were stocked in Woolworths (RIP) and other high street chains.

They are perhaps best remembered, however, for their low-priced compilation LPs – a fail-proof stocking filler.

I remember popping into my local Martin's newsagent and purchasing *Raiders of the Pop Charts* ('Buy Volume 1 Get Volume 2 FREE!') in 1982. It had a rather impressive tracklisting:

Side A

Madness – 'Our House'
Modern Romance – 'Best Years of Our Lives'
Haircut 100 – 'Love Plus One'
Clannad – 'Theme from *Harry's Game*'
Raw Silk – 'Do it to the Music'
The Chaps – 'Rawhide'
Incantation – 'Cacharpaya'
Fat Larry's Band – 'Zoom'

Side B

Culture Club – 'Do You Really Want to Hurt Me?'
Pretenders – 'Back on the Chain Gang'
Japan – 'Nightporter'

Heaven 17 – 'Let Me Go'
Tight Fit – 'Fantasy Island'
Dave Stewart & Barbara Gaskin – 'Johnny Rocco'
Toni Basil – 'Mickey'

Side C

Kid Creole and the Coconuts – 'Annie, I'm Not Your
    Daddy'
Yazoo – 'Only You'
Lene Lovich – 'It's You, Only You (Mein Schmerz)'
The Beat – 'I Confess'
Toto Coelo – 'I Eat Cannibals'
Precious Little – 'The On and On Song'
Whodini – 'Magic's Wand'
Pale Fountains – 'Thank You'

Side D

Shakin' Stevens – 'Give Me Your Heart Tonight'
Simple Minds – 'Someone Somewhere (In
    Summertime)'
Robert Palmer – 'Some Guys Have All the Luck'
UB40 – 'So Here I Am'
Gregory Isaacs – 'Night Nurse'
Morissey Mullen – 'Bladerunner'
Kids from Fame – 'Starmaker'

This was followed one year later by *Chart Encounters of the Hit Kind*, which repeated the successful formula. Ronco also released a series of soundtracks including *Stardust*, *That'll Be The Day* and *The Stud*, as well as hits collections from The Monkees, Percy Faith, Lena Martell, Joe Longthorne, Lonnie Donegan and even the official *Russ Abbot's Madhouse* album. Oh, and the obligatory selection of Christmas compilations.

Their brash but effective ads were one of the mainstays of Christmas television viewing for more than a decade, but they filed for bankruptcy in 1984 and were never heard from again.

Dodo Rating: 🦤🦤🦤🦤🦤

Uncle Remus Play-Kits

Uncle Remus himself was no relation to his namesake, the 'Zip-a-dee-doo-dah' chap from the Disney movie. He was, instead, a benevolent grandfather cartoon character. His small pocket-money craft-and-art sets were sold widely during the '70s and '80s, but by the time the '90s came round they had vanished without a trace. Today they are largely forgotten.

They were often sold from standalone spinners in toy shops and newsagents, which would display a variety of kits that would keep kids entertained for an hour or so at weekends or during the school holidays. They were also the ideal stocking filler and, thanks to their low price, the sort of gift you could buy for your mates at school.

The range covered everything from finger-puppet kits to activity books, collections of stickers to kits that enabled you to make a picture of a tiger out of pieces of felt. Simple, uncomplicated, but remarkably effective. And cheap.

Similar types of sets are sold at service stations and bargain shops today, but none prompt quite the same nostalgic-twang of the heartstrings as these classics of yesteryear.

Dodo Rating: 🐦🐦🐦🐦🐦

Pocketeers

Pocketeers were pocket-sized (as the name suggests) mechanical games that successfully delighted kids for a few short years before their silicon chip rendered them outdated and obsolete.

Licensed from Tomy in Japan, they launched in the UK in 1975 with eight different games:

Cup Final. A very simple bagatelle (or pinball-type) game in which you used flippers to try to get small ball-bearings into the goal by avoiding the keeper.

Fruit Machine. Pulling a paddle at the side caused classic fruit-machine symbols to rotate at random; pre-printed scores on the front panel indicated how well you had done when the fruit stopped.

Crossbow. Rather than being self-contained games, some of the early Pocketeers had removable parts. In this one the plastic box doubled up as a target, at which the player shot with a tiny crossbow and rubber-tipped arrows.

Blowpipe. Essentially the same idea as Crossbow, but with a blowpipe. It was important not to inhale too deeply before blowing.

The Derby. A classic Pocketeer format, which was also rebranded as other similar games, including Grand Prix and Speedway. Four tiny horses were hurled around a course by rotating a little disc with your finger. There was presumably a magnet underneath that propelled the horses along. There was no real skill involved, and the winner was always pretty random.

Pinball. Actually more like pachinko or bagatelle, with balls being pinged through a series of holes and pins into scoring zones.

Golf. A miniature, one-hole crazy-golf kit that you took out of the box and assembled.

They appear incredibly primitive by today's standards, yet they were actually, for the time, quite ingenious little creations. New titles were released on a regular basis, ending up with 46 on the market. As they developed, they became slightly more complex, including timers, two-player versions and even branded Smurf games. However, once the first hand-held computer games hit the market, Pocketeers were effectively dead and buried.

Dodo Rating: 🐦🐦🐦🐦🐦

Board Games

Here are just some of the board games that are no longer manufactured, either because the nation's children grew out of them or the companies went bust, or, in some cases, because the games were just too bloody complicated to play:

Bermuda Triangle. Navigate your shipping fleet safely across the Bermuda Triangle without a spooky magnetic cloud sweeping your ships away.

Coppit. 'Fast and frantic fun for all the family. Can you get all your pieces home before your opponents?' This was a bit like Ludo but with conical counters that you could slot over other players' pieces thereby sending them back to the start.

Escalado. A tabletop horse-racing game. Escalado involved betting on small metal horses, which were connected to a winding mechanism that recreated a race with a random winner each time. Hugely popular from the 1920s right through to the '70s.

Escape from Colditz. Actually devised by an ex-Colditz prisoner, this strategy game allowed you to play as either a prisoner or a convict.

The Garden Game. This first appeared in 1980 and required players to collect seed cards and plant them in beds, hopefully avoiding nasty board-game weather and other green-fingered calamities. Copies in good condition are now highly collectible.

Halma. A sort of cross between chess and draughts, this board game was around for decades before it fell out of favour in the '70s and is now largely forgotten.

'Owzthat'. A simple cricket game played with two metal six-sided rollers, one a traditional die, the other containing the scores 1, 2, 3, 4 and 6 plus an OWZTHAT side. Players would roll and keep a running total of their score until OWZTHAT came up, at which point the second roller would come into play, with different outcomes – caught, stumped, not out, etc. – determining the result of each appeal.

Stratego. A slightly more colourful adaptation of *L'Attaque* (or Capture the Flag), which was TV-advertised in the 1970s and sold well for a while. There was a competing version known as Tri-Tactics that was also a bestseller.

Totopoly. A hugely-popular horse training and racing board game that sold well from the 1940s through to the '70s.

Up Periscope. Three-dimensional battleships game in which your map was vertical and you pegged your ships to it, trying to work out where your opponent had stashed their fleet by use of a very primitive periscope. Actually far more fun than it sounds.

Dodo Rating: 🐥🐥🐥🐥

Gift Vouchers

I think the days of the brand-specific voucher are numbered. Let me explain.

When HMV went bust in 2013 the administrators refused to accept HMV gift vouchers for a while. This prompted outrage from those with unspent vouchers sitting in drawers. The same happened with Comet and Jessops, and there have been other similar examples in recent years.

So many people have had their fingers burnt, who will now be very wary of handing over cash for a piece of paper that may prove worthless a few weeks later. Some will continue, of course, but I think companies will sell fewer of them and I am so sure of this I will wager my £10 Borders and £20 Woolworths vouchers on it. Any takers?

These high-profile cases prove the value of the old universal voucher. If the old-style EMI record tokens still existed it wouldn't matter if your local HMV had closed down, you could spend them somewhere else. Assuming you could find somewhere else, of course. The iconic EMI record token was a music-industry led initiative that allowed anyone to walk into a record shop, buy tokens to pretty much any value they desired and then send them in a gift card to someone else in the UK who could then exchange them in *their* local record shop for an album of their choice. It was a great system because a) it meant that a granny who loved Richard Clayderman could give the gift of music to her grandson who liked Dinosaur Jr., and

b) they could be used in any branch of any record chain or any independent. They were universal and it worked extremely well.

But this rock 'n' roll utopia came to an end once WH Smith, HMV and the like realised that they would be better off producing their own vouchers which could only be used in their stores. This was a death sentence for the humble EMI token, which was a real shame because, recently, some of these newer tokens have proven not to be worth the paper they were printed on.*

Anyway, even if I am wrong about this we are definitely nearing the end of the paper voucher. Gift cards are the thing now, credit card-like bits of plastic that allow you to load them with cash, topping up when required or throwing away once finished. Give it a few years and there won't be any paper ones in sight.

Dodo Rating:

---

* *I discuss the demise of the record token at length in* 21st Century Dodos, *if you're interested.*

Soap on a Rope

Rarely did a 1970s Christmas go by without at least one person in the family unwrapping a soap on a rope, a product that I am pretty sure was only invented because it created a mildly-amusing rhyme, which is quite wonderful, when you think about it.

It was, however, a genuinely practical gift. It consisted of a bar of soap through which a loop of rope has been threaded, and was intended to be placed over the tap or shower head or the bather's wrist so that the soap wouldn't slip out of their hand and vanish beneath the bubbles only to cause serious accidents when trodden on.

For some reason, possibly because of the silly name or perhaps the jokes about prison showers, soap on a rope became a bit of a joke item and is nowadays more likely to be given as a novelty gift than a serious one.

Suggested by Nasim Marie Jafry

Dodo Rating: 🐦🐦🐦🐦

Annuals

Yearly annuals, alongside the nostalgia market – of which this book is a shameless contributor – have kept alive a number of comics of yesteryear whose weekly editions have long since gone off to the great newsagent in the sky (*The Dandy* being the latest casualty).

However, there are also many annuals that lots of us received during Christmases past that have not seen the light of day for decades.

How many can you remember?

Tiger Tim, Rainbow, Radio Fun, Rover, Hotspur, Wizard, Playbox, School Friend, Film Fun, Girls' Crystal, Jackie, Tammy, Mandy, June, Jinty, Princess, Boys' Own, The Lion, Playhour, Look-in, Bunty, Look and Learn, Cheeky, Whizzer and Chips, Buster, Twinkle, Sparky, Jack and Jill, and *Beezer.*

If you still have any lying around you might want to dig them out. They are worth a small fortune.

Dodo Rating: 🐦🐦🐦🐦🐦

CARDS &
DECORATIONS

Tinsel

Controversial stuff, tinsel.

For some the festive season hasn't officially started until miles of tinsel is strung up around their tree, or over their mantelpiece and any other available surface.

For others it is a cheap and tacky symbol of Christmas past, out of date and out of fashion. You won't catch Kirsty Allsop or Cath Kidston sticking tinsel up around their houses. No way.

The debate continues.

It is also worth remembering that it used to kill kids.

OK, that might be taking it a bit far, but it's true that during the '50s and '60s tinsel was often made from lead foil, a substance now known to be more than a little poisonous – hardly the sort of material to be filling the house with.

But it didn't start out that way. Tinsel originated in the early 17th century. Back then it was made of thin strands of silver, thus was an expensive decoration used only by the rich. It was – and this seems to have been largely forgotten in the mists of time – designed to look like icicles. Modern tinsel comes in many bright colours, is made from PVC and is about as far away from an icicle as it is possible to get.

Tacky or traditional? Your view on this may determine how high a dodo rating tinsel receives. There is still plenty of it around, but you used to find it in *every* home come Christmas time. Not any more.

Dodo Rating: 🐦🐦🐦

Advent Calendars

Although I can understand the appeal, especially to a child, of waking up every morning in December and shoving a piece of chocolate down your gob, I nonetheless fear for the future of the more traditional, sweet-free Advent calendar. You know the ones: quite cardboardy, little perforated window, cute little picture behind each number. They are still around, but they are a lot less common than they once were; I had some trouble finding one for my kids last Christmas, although that might have had more to do with the fact that Woolworths no longer exists.

Traditional Advent calendars were at their most popular in the Victorian era, when they would often be of a most elaborate construction. More recently they have become less ornate, and are usually made up of a large festive illustration, perhaps a snowy landscape or some such image, with pictures behind each window that rarely bear any relation to those on the front. In fact, sometimes you couldn't identify the small Advent image at all – 'Is this a mouse or an elf, Daddy?', 'I am not sure, son, it might be a potato.'

It is widely accepted that Advent calendars originated in Germany. Or maybe Austria. One of the two. No other country claims to have invented them, so we can let those Germanic neighbours fight it out among themselves. Before the advent, as it were, of Advent calendars, the run up to Christmas was marked by either the lighting of candles, hence the thing of beauty that was the *Blue Peter* Advent crown, or by chalk markings on the fireplace.

It has dawned on me, however, that Advent calendars don't actually follow the true days of Advent at all, Advent being the four weeks leading up to Christmas, as marked by Christians and their churches. A 'real' Advent calendar would often have to start in late November to be accurate, but, thinking about it, that might be a few chocolates too many as far as dentists are concerned.

Suggested by Darren Goldsmith

Dodo Rating: 🐤🐤🐤

Paper Chains

Whole mornings in school licking sticky-backed paper until your tongue went numb, all to make a paper chain with which to decorate your classroom. Simple, cheap, disposable.

And covered in spit.

Suggested by Jo Hockey and Jon Simmonds

Dodo Rating: 🐤🐤🐤🐤

Paper Decorations

Complementing the home-made paper chains were an array of fold-out and concertinaed paper decorations you could buy from the shops. These were often made of crepe paper so flimsy that no amount of honeycomb construction could render them sturdy, thus they spent the whole of Christmas swinging from side to side in the slightest breeze.

Now quite rare, although sightings may be made at your local nursing home or taxi cab office.

Suggested by Darren Goldsmith

Dodo Rating: 🐤🐤🐤🐤

Cards That Won't Stand Up

Do you remember these? Please email me if you do so that I know I didn't imagine them.

These were the most budget of all budget Christmas cards, and I am sure I received a bunch of them during the '70s, more often than not from schoolmates or very elderly relatives. They were distinctive in two ways. The first way was the clichéd photographic image on the front: a bauble on a tree, a robin, a holly bush, a snowy church, a stained-glass window, a fireplace or some variation thereof. The other was the fact that they were printed on such low-quality, thin card that they could barely hold their own weight; once you added a thin layer of ink for the greeting they simply couldn't take it any more and would collapse as soon as placed on the mantelpiece.

The envelope was usually more substantial than the card itself. But not by much.

I haven't seen any of these for ages, so I assume they were a phenomenon specific to that decade. Perhaps the entire world's stock blew away when someone sneezed or something. Anyway, I am pleased to see the back of them and I am delighted to pronounce them extinct.*

Dodo Rating: 🐦🐦🐦🐦🐦

Although, if any of you have one lying around, I would gladly take it off your hands. You know, for old time's sake.

Handwritten Cards

In *21st Century Dodos* I went off on one about the decline of handwritten letters. Shortly after, I, perhaps rather foolishly, offered on my blog to write a postcard to anyone on the planet who wanted one.* I had hundreds of responses and spent the best part of a month writing dozens of cards each night. The writer's cramp was horrible, but the sense of worth, the achievement of having done it, was considerable. The sight of something written by hand in among the bills and junk mail brought many people a tiny moment of joy, just as it did to me when they replied.

The handwritten letter definitely qualifies as a dodo, not quite extinct but certainly endangered, and I fear the same may soon be the case for the handwritten Christmas card.

Think about it, how many people do you know who proudly announce via Facebook or email 'I have decided not to send any Christmas cards this year. It is kinder to the environment not to use all that paper so I am making a donation to charity and sending an e-card instead'? Companies and organisations seem to do it as a matter of course, which doesn't really bother me as no one wants a Christmas card from their bank or optician, but the

---

And I will do the same for any of you who want me to. Just email me at 21stcenturydodos@gmail.com with your address, and I will send you something in the post.

amount of people, real people, doing it is starting to trouble me. Is it really that hard to write a bloody card?

I do realise that posting anything these days is an expensive pastime, especially since the Royal Mail introduced their ridiculous small letter/large letter/thin letter/fat letter/parcel rules, but I implore you: write something in your own hand to the ones you love. It shows you care more than almost anything else could. It shows more thought, more consideration, more personal feeling than an email with a picture of a robin on the front, even if it does start snowing when you click on it.

Dodo Rating:

Long Addresses

… And, if you are sending cards this year, how many of them will have incredibly convoluted addresses on the front of the envelope? By which I do not mean:

> Steve Stack
> 17 Dodo Lane
> Newtown
> Middlesex
> England
> UK
> Europe
> The World
> The Solar System
> Etc.

Which we all used to do at school.
   No, I mean:

> Steve Stack
> 17 Dodo Lane
> Off High Street
> Newtown
> Nr. Brentford
> Middlesex
> DD0 0DX

Do we really think, in this day and age, that the postman needs to be told that Dodo Lane is off the High Street, or that Newtown is near Brentford? Of course we don't, because of course he doesn't, this is just a tradition harking back to pre-computerised days. All the postie actually needs is a house number and a postcode – a letter could reach me if it were addressed to Stack, 27, DD0 0DX.* We don't need the other stuff at all.

But I rather like it and I hope it stays around; I fear our addresses will get shorter and shorter until they are just a grouping of letters and numbers, or perhaps a QR code.

That's technology for you – that's progress. Gone are the antiquated days of long addresses, cheap first and second class stamps, two postal deliveries a day and even a delivery on Christmas day …

Dodo Rating: 🐦🐦

Although it wouldn't, because that's not my address.

Christmas Post

Yes, you read that last entry correctly, we used to get a postal delivery on Christmas Day. This only stopped in 1960 in England and Wales.

In Scotland it kept going till 1966. They are far more festive up there.

Hard to imagine it now, of course. I doubt we'd welcome the intrusion or that the postman would fancy having to work that day.

Although he'd stand more chance of getting a Christmas box.

Dodo Rating: 🐦🐦🐦🐦🐦

Angel Hair

For much of the '70s and '80s, tinsel had a challenger in the race to decorate the nation's Christmas trees. Angel hair was a peculiar, well, hair-like substance usually made out of soft-spun glass (though it was perfectly safe to handle and hang on your tree). It could sometimes look as if Santa had crashed into your tree on his way out of the house, leaving tufts of his beard behind (at least, I hope it was his beard).

It is still manufactured and used today – very popular in Germany actually – but is pretty thin on the ground over here in the UK.

Suggested by Jess Ruston and Emma Wayland

Dodo Rating: 🦤🦤🦤🦤

Candles on Trees

Before the days of fairy lights, people used to put candles on their trees. Actual candles. With flames and everything.

Can you imagine the conniptions this would cause for the Health and Safety Brigade today?

Almost tempting to bring them back, isn't it? Just to annoy them.

Dodo Rating:

Thank You Letters

Another victim of this age of electronic communication is the humble thank you letter. This short note from a child to a relative or family friend, many of whom they have rarely or never met, showing gratitude for the Parker pen, record token or other unwanted gift, is a Christmas tradition that taxes both the sender (most kids need to be bullied into sitting down and writing them) and the recipient (making sense of bad handwriting and even worse spelling), but which, at its heart, is a precious acknowledgement of a simple act of kindness.

Some people still write them, of course, but the duty can just as well be dispatched with an email or a Facebook message, both of which are faster, easier and enable spell check. However, they are much less personal. This is yet another way that handwritten communication is rapidly vanishing from our lives.

Dodo Rating: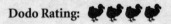

FESTIVE FUN

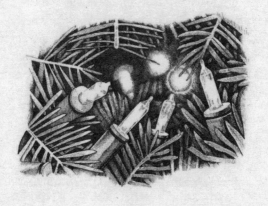

Snowball Fights in
the Playground

Nowadays, schools are so obsessed with health and safety, and with not getting sued, that no remotely dangerous activity is permitted on school premises. Never mind that one of the most important lessons children can learn in life is how to assess risk – they will have to practice that in their own time.

So, no conkers, no games of knuckles, no holding your breath till your face turns blue.

And, no snowball fights.

Not that many kids would get a chance to start a snowball fight at school, seeing as most of them close at the first sign of a snowflake.

All together now: It was never like this in my day!

Dodo Rating: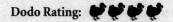

Christmas Singles

Do you know when we last had a Christmas No.1 single that had any sort of Christmas theme? Or what it was? Go on, have a guess – and don't scan down the page to see the answer! I suspect you'll be surprised, perhaps a little bit horrified.

In a world where digital downloads have seen the near-death of the physical single as a format, you'd be forgiven for thinking that getting the Christmas No.1 spot isn't such a big deal anymore. But it *is* a big deal. The Christmas No. 1 is still the biggest-selling song of the year, and it can make a hell of a lot of money, which is why Simon Cowell works his Svengali backside off every year to try and secure it. And, since he began his domination of the Christmas charts, most other artists have stopped bothering to challenge him, with the only serious competition being a protest involving a Rage Against the Machine song with a chorus of 'F*** you, I won't do what you tell me' or the occasional charity record (which Simon will always say he'd love to see go to number one, whilst probably actually seething inside). Worst of all, Cowell insists that the winning *X-Factor* artist schlocks out a cover that has nothing to do with the festive season whatsoever.

Today, no one of any note bothers to write and record Christmassy singles. Don't believe me? Pick up any Christmas compilation on sale this year and count the number of songs written in this century. If it's more than five, I'll eat my hat.

Before the days of reality talent shows, many credible, and admittedly many not so credible, artists were eager to record something festive and join the race to the number one spot; the very best of them have now become part of the fabric of Christmas itself. You'd be hard-pressed to recognise Jona Lewie if you passed him in the street, or name any of his albums, but I bet you can hum along to 'Stop the Cavalry'. Like me, you might cringe at the vocal gymnastics of Mariah Carey, but I'd wager you also, like me, know all the words to 'All I Want for Christmas is You', annoying though it may be. 'Merry Christmas Everybody', 'I Wish it Could be Christmas Every Day', 'Last Christmas', the classic festive tunes are many, but none of them are recent.*

Will this change? It is hard to say for sure, but there do seem to be some fairy lights at the end of the tunnel. Viewers appear to be tiring of Cowell's stage-managed search for a star, especially as most of them sink without a trace after a year. So, perhaps some artists may be tempted to give him a run for his money in the years ahead. Who knows, if you are reading this in a few years' time, there may be no *X-Factor* whatsoever.

I can think of no finer Christmas present to the nation.

Oh, and the answer to the question I posed at the beginning of this entry? 'Saviour's Day' by Cliff Richard in 1990. Unless you want to count the re-recording of 'Do

---

* *Entertainment journalist James King discusses this subject in far more detail in his excellent ebook* It's Christmas! Whatever Happened to the Christmas Single?

They Know It's Christmas?' by Band Aid 20 in 2004, something which most of us would rather forget.

Dodo Rating: 🐦🐦🐦🐦

Shopping in Woolworths

If there was one shop that summed up Christmas shopping, it was Woolworths. You could get everything you needed for your Yuletide celebrations there: cards, records, videos, books, toiletries, pens, decorations, pans for cooking the turkey, festive napkins, toys, jigsaws, clothes, pick 'n' mix, video recorders, chocolate selection boxes, teddy bears, cameras, wrapping paper, computer games, stereo systems, crockery, chocolate coins, batteries, party invitations, ice cube trays, fizzy pop, measuring jugs, turkey basters, cutlery, stockings, television listing magazines, gift vouchers, televisions, giant Toblerones, cookery books, *Now That's What I Call Christmas*, perfume, aftershave gift sets, soap on a rope, crackers, games consoles, colouring books, candles, Tupperware, lottery tickets, footballs, bouncy balls, annuals, sticker sets, tablecloths, jars, cake tins, indoor fireworks, party poppers, Terry's Chocolate Oranges and dustbin bags.

There is nowhere you can get all of that stuff today.

I miss Woolworths.

Dodo Rating: 🐦🐦🐦🐦🐦

TV Shows With More Than 10 Million Viewers

Did you know that 2012 was the first year since records began that no Christmas programme, not a single one, was watched by more than 10 million viewers?

In the '70s, top-rated shows over the festive period would often pull in audiences in excess of 20 million, but from the '80s onwards viewing figures have tumbled all year round and that includes Christmas. This was, at first, because of the increasing number of channels available – Channel Four came along, then there was Channel Five, and eventually satellite and cable TV entered most homes – but of late, it's down to the ability to record shows onto a hard drive at the touch of a button, and the fact that you can watch pretty much anything you want online days or weeks after it was first broadcast, meaning that there is little need to watch television *as it happens*. The shared viewing experience is on the decline. People will watch things when they want, not when the stations schedule them, and the people's choices are legion.

There are probably more people watching television now than in the '70s, but they are watching a thousand different things, from the *Dr Who* Christmas special to *Man vs. Food* to 'Today's Special Value' on QVC. As a result, it is highly unlikely that any programme broadcast on Christmas Day will get more than 10 millions viewers ever again.

Moreover, the decline is speeding up. In 2010, nearly 16 million people watched the *EastEnders* episode broadcast on December 25th, making it the most viewed show that day. In 2012, that programme was still number one in the rankings, but it took only 9.4 million viewers to put it there.

Dodo Rating:

White Christmases

If you speak to anyone over the age of 40 about white Christmases they will probably rattle on about how there were lots of them when they were young but you hardly get them any more. I know I do if the subject ever comes up.

But this is all nonsense. Utter balderdash.

There were only seven – yes, seven – white Christmases in England* during the entire 20th Century. And, though we've had two in the 21st, they remain quite rare, happening much less frequently than in ancient times (from the 16th up to the 19th century, they were extremely common).

Perhaps the reason for our false memory is that for a white Christmas to be declared there has to be snowfall *on* Christmas Day. If you are standing in ten-foot drifts from the day before, but no snowflakes appear on the 25th, then it isn't a white Christmas. So there. Thus, we probably do recall a fair few festive periods with snow on the ground, but many of them would not have counted.

Global warming seems to be playing havoc with our weather of late so who knows if the instances of snow on Christmas Day are going to go up or down. For now, they are pretty scarce so they deserve a place in this book.

Dodo Rating: 🦤🦤🦤

---

* *Scotland has had quite a few more. Congratulations, Scottish readers!*

Disney Time

For well over a decade, *Disney Time* was essential family viewing at Christmas. During the '70s and early '80s, it was broadcast every year, nearly always on Christmas Eve, Christmas Day or Boxing Day. It featured a celebrity presenting a series of clips from Disney films.

These celebrity presenters included Rolf Harris, Paul and Linda McCartney, Paul Daniels, Lenny Henry, Jimmy Tarbuck, Windsor Davies, Felicity Kendal, Jim Davidson (that stalwart of family television), The Goodies, Tom Baker (in character as Doctor Who), Derek Nimmo and Harry Worth, as well as various *Blue Peter* presenters.

There was even a special episode broadcast to celebrate the wedding of Prince Charles and Lady Diana in 1981; it was hosted by Penelope Keith.

Disney Time was at its height in the years before video and DVD. At this time, the Disney company were very shrewd about their theatrical releases, showing the major movies – *Pinnochio*, *Jungle Book* etc. – only once every seven years in the cinema, so these compilation shows were the only way to hear the 'Bare Necessities' or 'Zip-a-dee-doo-dah' in those days. Quite why *Disney Time* stopped airing is unclear.

Suggested by Jonathan Pinnock

Dodo Rating: 🐤🐤🐤🐤🐤

Pages from Ceefax

When you were a kid, the whole point of Christmas was to wake up as early as possible so that you could dive into your presents and spend the rest of the day playing with them, breaking them, wearing out the batteries and annoying your parents while they tried to catch up on some much-needed sleep on the sofa.

In those days, of course, there was nothing on the TV in the wee morning hours apart from a selection of pages from Ceefax, the BBC's teletext service. Ceefax would happily scroll through news, weather, television listings, knitting patterns and sports results, while Acker Bilk or Mantovani chirped along in the background.

That peculiar combination of words, pictures and music was, for many, the true soundtrack to a Christmas morning.

Ceefax broadcast from 1974 right up until October 2012.

Dodo Rating:

January Sales

It may be hard to believe, but the January sales actually used to start in January. It was a tradition and, dare I suggest, quite a good one. Shops wanted to sell off their leftover stock from Christmas, but had the decency to allow us to finish the turkey carcass, polish off the last of the chocolates and finally get sick of sitting around the house with the family before they did so.

But the date started creeping forward. Shops in the high street began to launch their sales towards the end of December, and before you knew it they were kicking off on Boxing Day. I still remember the first time I saw posters in the window of Next proclaiming 'SALE STARTS BOXING DAY AT 6AM'. Six in the morning?! What sort of idiot would get up on the morning after Christmas just to buy a pair of jeans for half price? Then again, I heard reports of queues and a security guard having to let people in a small number at a time, so what do I know?

Nowadays many retailers start their sales before we even get to Christmas Day. Plenty of clothes shops are in full knockdown mode by mid-December. There is something rather depressing about this, but I am not sure why – there's nothing inherently wrong with being able to buy things cheap. I guess having January sales actually *in* January is just another Christmas tradition that has eroded away.

Suggested by Nasim Marie Jafry

Dodo Rating: 🐦🐦🐦🐦

Thanks

For doing all the work to actually turn this into a book: Corinna, Rachel and Alice.

For drawing the lovely pictures: Dave Cornmell. (Buy his book *364 Days of Tedium*, it is hilarious!)

For allowing me to go away and write it: Rhian, Ethan and Martha.

For coming up with ideas to fill the pages: Chris, Jo, Tim, Caroline, Vanessa, Paul, Jonathan, Trevor, Steve, Nasim, Jacqueline, Darren, Jon, Jess and Emma.

For making the effort to ensure my childhood Christmases were truly magical: Mum and Dad.

For all the tea and stuff: Kat.

Dodos Online

My obsession with dodos doesn't stop with the two books I have written on the subject. I bang on about them online all the time as well.

Facebook
www.facebook.com/21stcenturydodos

Come and say hello on the Facebook page where you will find articles, photos, links, discussions and competitions. Share your dodos with other readers and bother me with questions and comments.

Twitter
@dodoflip

Whenever I find anything dodo-related online, I will tweet a link. Feel free to follow.

Flipboard
@dodoflip

If you have the Flipboard app for your iPad or iPhone then follow my feed for a fantastic interactive Dodos magazine – images, videos and articles on all manner of endangered objects, both festive and otherwise.

Email
Or you can email me at:
21stcenturydodos@gmail.com

About the Author

Steve Stack is the pseudonym of a blogger and sometime journalist. He is the author of two previous books, *It Is Just You, Everything's Not Shit* and the precursor to this book, *21st Century Dodos*, both of which can probably still be found in bargain bookshops and Poundland if you wanted to add them to your toilet library. They are also available as specially priced (i.e. very cheap) ebooks if you are all very modern and own one of those new-fangled devices. If you want to contact Steve, you can drop him a line at 21stcenturydodos@gmail.com. You can also pay a visit to his blog at meandmybigmouth. typepad.com.

Please send him cake.

Thank you.

Did I mention my other book *21st Century Dodos*, available now as a real book, an ebook and an audio book? I can't remember …